VALLEY VIEW ELEMEN̄
ELLENSBURG, WA 989

MW00981945

DISCARD

People of the Middle Ages
PRINCESS

Melinda Lilly

Original illustrations by Cheryl Goettemoeller

Rourke

Publishing LLC
Vero Beach, Florida 32964

www.rourkepublishing.com

For Lyra

To My Darling Daughters, Laurena and Jade - C.G.

PICTURE CREDITS: Page 5, "Saint Margaret," from Prayer Book of Charles the Bold, Lieven van Lathem and Master of Mary of Burgundy (illuminators), and Nicolas Spierinc (scribe), originally completed by 1469, about 1480–1490, 12.4 x 9.2 cm., The J. Paul Getty Museum, Los Angeles; Page 6, miniature detail, "Philosophy Presenting the Seven Liberal Arts to Boethius," from *Miniatures and Border Cuttings from Boethius, Consolation de Philosophie*, Coëtivy Master (Henri de Vulcop?) illuminator, about 1460–1470, various sizes, The J. Paul Getty Museum, Los Angeles; Page 9, MS. Rawl. D. 591, fol. 21, courtesy of the Bodleian Library, University of Oxford; Page 10, "Markgraff Otto von Brandenburg," (Cod. Pal. Germ. 848, fol. 13r) from the *Codex Manesse*, courtesy of the University of Heidelberg; Page 13, "The Temperate and the Intemperate," a miniature from *Faits et Dits Memorables des Romains*, Master of the Dresden Prayer Book (illuminator), about 1475–1480, 17.5 x 19.4 cm., The J. Paul Getty Museum, Los Angeles; Page 14, "Hedwig and the New Convent, Nuns from Bamberg Settling at the New Convent of Trebnitz," from *Vita beatae Hedwigis, Life of the Blessed Hedwig*, by Court atelier of Duke Ludwig I of Liegnitz and Brieg (illuminator) and Nicolaus of Prussia (scribe), 1353, 34.1 x 24.8, The J. Paul Getty Museum, Los Angeles; Page 17, miniature of "The Marriage of Louis de Blois and Marie de France," from *Chroniques (Book 3)*, Master of the White Inscriptions (illuminator), about 1480, 48.2 x 35 cm., The J. Paul Getty Museum, Los Angeles; Page 25, "The Battle Between Arnault de Lorraine and His Wife Lydia," from *Fifteen Leaves from Histoire de Charles Martel*, Pol Fruit and Loyset Liédet (illuminators), and David Aubert (author and scribe), written 1463–1465, illuminated 1467–1472 or 1473, approximately 23 x 19 cm., The J. Paul Getty Museum, Los Angeles; Original art on cover and pages 18, 21, 22, 26, and 29 is by Cheryl Goettemoeller.

Cover illustration: A princess with her lap dog and open book. As a princess in the Middle Ages (years 500 to 1500) you may have been taught how to read and write.

Editor: Frank Sloan

Cover design by Nicola Stratford

Library of Congress Cataloging-in-Publication Data

Lilly, Melinda
    Princess / Melinda Lilly
      p. cm. — (People of the middle ages)
    Includes bibliographical references and index.
   Summary: Presents some of the details of the life of a princess or queen in Europe in the Middle Ages.
    ISBN 1-58952-231-1
     1. Women—History—Middle Ages, 500-1500—Juvenile literature. 2. Princesses—Europe—History—Juvenile literature. [1. Princesses. 2. Kings, queens, rulers, etc. 3. Women—History—Middle Ages, 500-1500. 4. Middle Ages. 5. Civilization, Medieval.] I. Title.

HQ1147 .E85 L56 2002   2001056508
305.42'092—dc21

Printed in the USA

CG/CG

Table of Contents

Fairy Tale or Real?

Flags wave! Trumpets blare! Servants bow as you lead your family into the castle. You are a princess in Europe. It is the **Middle Ages.** This period of time lasted from the year 500 to 1500.

You might tell stories of princesses and dragons to your sisters. Your life as a real princess, however, is not much like the fairy tales.

Tales of princesses and dragons come from the Middle Ages. Some believed the devil could turn himself into a dragon. Only the pure of heart could defeat him.

6

Rich and Royal

Because you are rich and royal, you can become powerful. Yet many people of your time think women are not as capable as men. Most women live under the "protection" of a father or husband. It's difficult for you to own land. Don't even try to leave the castle alone! It's not allowed.

However, if you are smart and lucky and a princess, you can take care of your country. Someday you can rule it.

These women are symbols of the subjects taught at a university of the Middle Ages. However, women were not allowed to attend university.

What You Need to Know

What do you need to learn as a princess? Sharpen up your adding and subtracting. Some day you will figure castle costs. Your mother may teach you to read and write. If you learn which plants can bring down a fever or heal a cut, you can help take care of your servants and family.

When you turn nine, you leave home. You live with another powerful family. There, you learn to spin and weave cloth, and run a large household.

An upper-class woman greets a man, writes a letter, and meets with nobles.

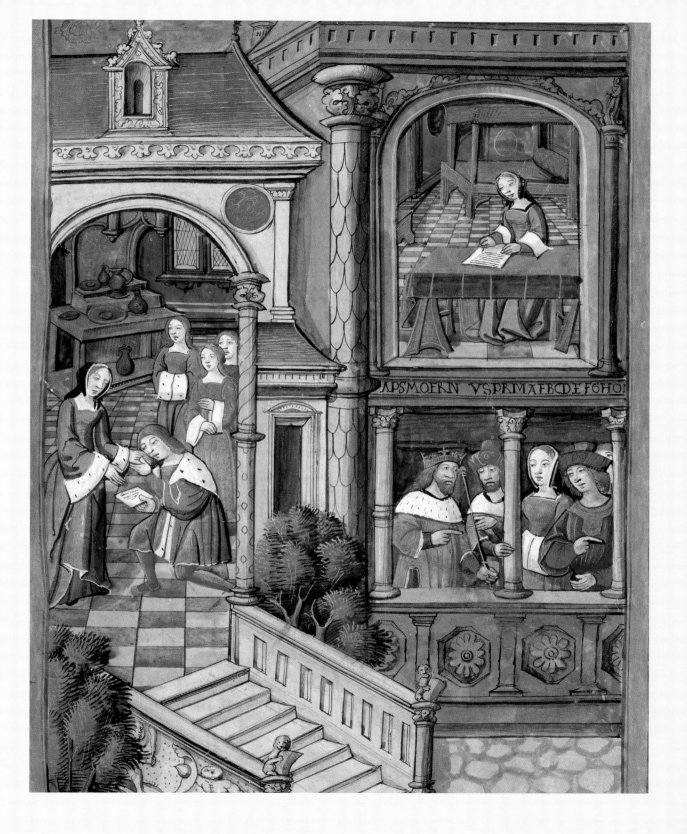

Fun Times

Thank goodness—princesses also need to know how to have fun! It's part of your job to entertain guests. On a sunny day, travel with them to a picnic. Weave flowers into your long hair. Play the lute and sing. You do know how to dance the **bassedance**, don't you?

After supper, you can beat a knight at chess or backgammon.

A woman plays chess with a knight as musicians entertain. This picture was made in the 1300s.

Mind Your Manners

When you become queen, if you insult the wrong person you could start a war! Follow these rules to be a Miss Manners of the Middle Ages: Don't talk too much. Walk, don't run or trot. When you sit, fold your hands in your lap unless you're playing with your lap dog.

That's not all. You're supposed to look good while being proper! Rub flour on your skin so you look pale as a tablecloth.

A bored noble girl (wearing veil) minds her manners as peasants relax at a nearby table.

13

Princess Nun

Love to learn? Want to avoid marriage to a less-than-charming prince? You might want to become a nun. You can spend your days studying and praying. Write books on religion and medicine. Copy **illuminated manuscripts**, books made by hand. Compose music and poetry. Play a harp and sing.

Perhaps you will run a school. Nuns are the best-educated women of the time.

(Top) A noblewoman oversees the construction of a convent for nuns. (Bottom) A noblewoman and nuns admire their new convent.

15

Getting Married

You're nine years old and not engaged to be married yet? Your parents could have chosen your groom for you while you were a little girl. Your royal marriage is not a love match. It is a bond between two families and countries.

You will not live with your husband until you are at least twelve years old and he is fourteen. However, your wedding can take place while you are a child.

This picture depicts a royal wedding of 1386. The groom was a young child at the time of the marriage. The artist decided to show both bride and groom as adults.

17

Her Royal Majesty

Today is your **coronation**. This ceremony changes you from a princess into a queen. You stand tall and hold a gold rod, or **scepter**. Its rich golden gleam is a symbol of your royal power.

During the church ceremony, you are touched with holy oil. This blessing shows the people you are meant to be queen. After many prayers, the crown is placed on your head. Hail to the Queen!

A proud princess becomes a queen.

19

Home Sweet . . . Castle!

Welcome home! You cross the bridge that spans the castle moat. As you enter the great hall, you cough. It's dark and smoky inside. Your small windows are covered with paper to keep out the cold air and a tree burns in your fireplace.

In this room, you eat, run your kingdom, and hold parties. Servants and visitors often sleep on the large tables. You sleep in a simple room upstairs.

A jester entertains during a meal in the great hall.

Running the Show

Hundreds of servants are paid to do as you tell them. It sounds great, doesn't it? However, running a castle is not easy. You oversee the servants. You hire and fire staff. You check the records to make sure you can pay your workers. You make political partnerships to increase your power.

Oh, no! The roasted peacocks have lost their feathers and guests are hungry. You figure out a way to present the meal in its feathered glory.

A queen instructs the cook on making dinner.

Taking Care of Business

When the king is away, you take care of his responsibilities as well as your own. You make laws. You settle arguments. You decide who should be taxed. You check on the lords and ladies who serve you.

When enemies attack, you leap on your white horse and lead your soldiers to victory! That's what Blanche of Castile did. She was a Spanish princess who ruled France in the 1200s.

24

Lydia of Burgundy prepares to lead her army into battle against her husband, Count Arnault of Lorraine. This page of an illuminated manuscript was created in the late 1400s.

Comment la guerre comença dentre le conte Arnault
de loheraine, et la contesse ludie sa femme fille du cont
fromont de lent ret de ses deux filz mennesier et lopes.
Istoire racompte que quant guivre nep
ueu du conte heruault du roy Anseys le
ienne du roy guerin de coulongne. Et d
conte mauuoysin eut prime la charite de
son oncle le conte heruault daler faire

Queen for a Day

Your day begins with dawn church service. Eat breakfast. Check that the nursemaid is taking care of the baby. Teach your older children their lessons.

Guests arrive today. Meet with the servants to make sure everything goes smoothly.

Welcome your guests. Chat politely during the ten-course meal. Convince the nobleman to your left that he needs to provide more soldiers for your army. Play **blindman's buff** with your guests. If you can remain charming after all that, you really are a queen!

Royals play blindman's buff.

27

Royal Treatment

You want your country to prosper. If you are a powerful queen, you work with other nobles to help your people. You carefully make decisions. Your choices will affect thousands.

It is your duty to give to the poor and support the arts. People write books for you. Singers make rhymes praising your wit. Talk about getting the royal treatment! Being queen can be pretty terrific.

A queen listens to a harpist.

Dates to Remember

476	Last Roman emperor overthrown (Romulus Augustulus)
500	Beginning of the Middle Ages
About 500	Castle of Chinon built (one of France's oldest castles)
1100–1300	Heyday of the Beguines; the only women's Christian movement entirely in the control of women
1188	Blanche of Castile born (Spanish princess and ruler of France)
1215	Magna Carta issued; this document limits the power of English royalty
1264	Thomas Aquinas, an important Christian thinker, begins *Summa Theologica*. In it, he argues that men are superior to women.
1364	Christine de Pisan, a leading woman writer of the Middle Ages, is born.
1500	End of the Middle Ages

Glossary

bassedance (BASS eh dans) — a dance of the Middle Ages with five steps

blindman's buff (BLINED manz BUF) — a game in which a blindfolded player tries to catch and guess the name of another player

coronation (kor uh NAY shun) — the crowning of a king or queen

illuminated manuscripts (ih LOO muh nayt ed MAN yeh skripts) — decorated books made by hand; many were made in the Middle Ages

Middle Ages (MID ul AY jez) — a time in European history that lasted from the year 500 to 1500

nobles (NO bulz) — people of high social class

scepter (SEP tur) — a rod carried in the hand by a royal to show his or her power

Index

Further Reading

Brooks, Polly Schoyer. *Queen Eleanor: Independent Spirit of the Medieval World: A Biography of Eleanor of Aquitaine.* Houghton Mifflin Company, 1999.

Gravett, Christopher. *Eyewitness: Castle.* DK Publishing, 2000.

MacDonald, Fiona. *Women in Medieval Times.* NTC/Contemporary Publishing Company, 2000.

Websites to Visit

Explore a castle:
   www.nationalgeographic.com/castles/enter.html
Art of Illuminated Manuscripts of the Middle Ages:
   www.bnf.fr/enluminures/aaccueil.htm
Middle Ages site created by fourth and fifth grade students
   www.kyrene.k12.az.us/schools/brisas/sunda/ma/mahome.htm

About the Author

Melinda Lilly is the author of several children's books. Some of her past jobs have included editing children's books, teaching pre-school, and working as a reporter for *Time* magazine. She is the author of *Around The World With Food & Spices* also from Rourke.